CLEAN & SIMPLE **CARDS**™

Contents

Color

Pattern

Texture & Dimension

Letter to Readers

I have had countless people tell me, "You make 'clean and simple' look so easy." While I was sharing some cards on my blog, someone once made the comment that my cards are "non-intimidating."

From that point on, I knew my goal: to create and share cards that were not only easy on the budget but easy for others to re-create in a short amount of time. I also want people to realize that "easy" is OK. The fact that something is simple in appearance doesn't mean that no thought went into its design.

It appears to me that clean and simple card designs may be among the easiest to create, and at the same time, the most struggled-with design style of recent times. While the definition of the style may vary from person to person, the basic ideas of "less is more" and "white space is your friend" remain the same. My goal with *Clean & Simple Cards* is to show you how easy it really can be.

I do not want to simply teach you to copy a card step-by-step or use the latest and greatest products. The ultimate goal of this book is to equip you with the basic theories and techniques used in clean and simple card designs. By looking past the themes and products used and focusing on the way the cards are designed, you will gain information that will stand the test of time and become a go-to reference for years to come.

As you look through this book, I challenge you to look beyond the cards and the products and see how the design theory and techniques are put to use. In the back of the book, you will learn how to go even further with the ideas presented by looking at each card as a blueprint for design and converting it to your own unique design.

—Tami

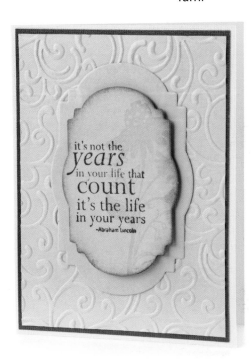

Designer Bio

Tami Mayberry is a wife and mother of five from the state of Missouri. She has created hundreds of cards and has written articles for *CardMaker* since its premier issue in May 2005.

Tami has created cards, scrapbook pages and altered-art designs for a variety of Annie's publications, including three books of her own.

When she is not working on designs and articles for our publications, you can find Tami creating special projects for various craft-product manufacturers and working on her graphic design skills as an illustrator for Gina K. Designs.

Visit Tami on her blog at *http://tamimayberry.blogspot.com*.

Clean & Simple Basics

The most dominant element in a design is known as the **focal point**. The focal point of any card is the component that receives the most emphasis, typically the greeting or main image. The first step in a well-designed card is to decide what the focal point will be. This will be the whole of what the card should say to the recipient.

Composition, the arrangement of elements, is a key factor in effectively spotlighting the focal point of a card. While the **Rule of Thirds** is commonly used in the composition of photography, it is a powerful tool when designing clean and simple cards as well. The Rule of Thirds makes use of the theory that the human eye is easily drawn to certain areas of a design. When using the Rule of Thirds, imagine the card base being divided into nine equal sections using two vertical and two horizontal lines. The four points where these lines intersect are the strongest focal points. The lines themselves are the second strongest focal points. When choosing the location of elements, position the most important elements, or focal points, along the lines or near the points at which they intersect.

Another popular version of the Rule of Thirds is sometimes referred to as the **Zone Method**.

When using the Zone Method, the project is divided into three equal sections either horizontally or vertically. Design elements are then situated within one or two of the divisions with the strongest horizontal section being the bottom section (left card) and the far right as the most visual of the vertical sections (right card).

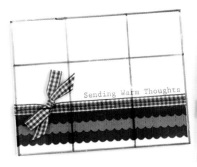

When starting out with the Rule of Thirds, a great tool to have on hand is a piece of acetate the size of a common card base, which has been marked with the grid pattern. This can be placed over the design to aid in the placement of elements. The easiest way to create a grid like this is to print out a grid the desired size and trace it onto the acetate with a permanent marker. ***Note:*** *For a free downloadable grid, visit http:// tamimayberry.blogspot.com.*

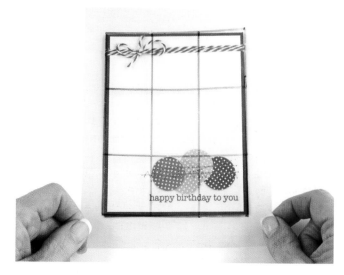

When deciding the location of the focal point, it is also important to consider the use of space. One of the most popular elements in clean and simple card design is the use of **white space**. While many clean and simple cards are white, this actually has nothing to do with the term *white space*. Every design has what is known as *positive space* and *negative space*. Positive space is that which contains the focal image or other embellishments. Negative space is everything else, or white space. This is the area devoid of visual elements, where the eye can rest. When a card contains a considerable amount of white space, it gives a clean and uncluttered feel, thus the "clean" in the term *clean and simple*. Learning to make use of this unfilled space and looking at it as part of the actual design is probably one of the most important—and, many times, most difficult—concepts to grasp in this type of card design.

be created in a variety of ways such as straight, zigzag, curved, diagonal or circular. The lines can also vary in thickness and design. The main factor is not the shape of the line but the fact that it is used to lead the eye to the card's focal image.

The circle of gems draws the eye to the center of the card and to the greeting.

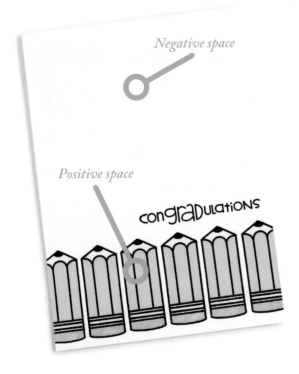

Negative space

Positive space

conGraDulatioNs

The red-and-white twine creates a vertical line that leads the eye to the greeting tag.

After deciding on the location of the card's focal point, the next step to consider is the use of **lines**. One of the earliest concepts taught in mathematics is that a line represents the path between two points. Lines signify motion and direction. When viewing a card, lines are the natural succession of how the eye is drawn across the design. The lines are many times portrayed through the use of embellishments or fine details. Lines can be formed through items like ribbon, scored lines, gems or even arrows. Lines can

The horizontal ribbon line moves the eye across the card to the brad and sentiment.

At this point, you want to answer the following questions about your card:

What do I want the card to "say" to the recipient?

Where will the focal point be located?

How will the viewer get to that point?

Now that the basic design layout has been determined, it's time for the fun part of adding the details. Obviously, the focal point will be the highlight of the design and the one that receives the most emphasis. There are a variety of ways to create and emphasize a focal point. Some of the most popular techniques are use of bright or contrasting color, pops of color, large or detailed images or surrounding the focal point with white space to make it stand out.

When deciding on the details of a card, interest can also be added through use of repetition, color, patterns and texture. These elements can be applied not only to the focal point but many times to the lines and white space as well.

Repetition of design elements creates interest through the use of a repeated component. The most attention-grabbing repetition occurs when there is variation in the chosen element. This could mean using a shape such as a circle for multiple components but varying the size and/or color throughout the design. It could mean using the same stamp image but stamping it in a variety of colors. The same greeting in different fonts would also be a good example of using varied repetition. The important factor when using repetition to create an appealing design is to use the chosen feature in a variety of ways.

Color is an important factor when adding detail to a card design. Like the focal image, the colors chosen are very important in conveying the desired message. Color can be added through papers, embellishments, inks, paints, markers and more. A color wheel can be a valuable tool when choosing colors. Colors can many times even be chosen based on the patterned paper being used.

Patterns can add interest to a design. Pattern can be incorporated into a design through the use of things such as printed papers, stamps, embellishments and

embossing. Embossed patterns are a great way to add both interest and texture. Patterns can also be an effective way to incorporate the use of lines.

Texture encompasses both the look and feel of the card. Texture adds depth and appeal to a design. In addition, it can also be a good way to pull in the use of repetition and patterns. Even so-called non-textured designs contain a texture. They are smooth, which in reality is a texture. Texture can be represented through cardstock texture, fibers, 3-D elements, embossing and more. Texture is very effective in creating the feel of a card. For example, a smooth or linen texture can be elegant and refined. When striving for a more outdoorsy or masculine feel, a natural element such as jute or twine might be used.

For more examples of how these design elements are put to use, be sure and watch for tips throughout the book. ●

Birthday Celebration

Design by Tami Mayberry

Materials

Core'dinations cardstock:
  snowflake, nightfall
Core'dinations David Tutera Greetings
  Combo white die-cut panel
Want2Scrap self-adhesive rhinestones:
  orange, turquoise, hot pink
Corner rounder punch
SCRAPBOOK ADHESIVES BY 3L™: adhesive
  foam squares, adhesive runner

1. Form a 5½ x 4¼-inch card from white cardstock. Round upper corners.

2. Cut a 5¼ x 4-inch piece from black cardstock; round all corners. Center and adhere to card front.

3. Trim "happy birthday" die-cut panel to 5¼ x 4 inches; round all corners. Embellish panel with rhinestones as shown. Attach panel to card front using foam squares. ●

tip

Use a cluster of three multicolored gems to add a pop of color to a black–and–white card.

Embellishments in sets of three are more appealing to the eye. Multiple colors add to the effect.

Believe in Your Dreams

Design by Latisha Yoast

Materials

Gina K. Designs white cardstock
Lawn Fawn Flutter By stamp set
Imagine Crafts/Tsukineko Memento
   tuxedo black ink pad
Copic® markers: V06, V09, Y08, YR12
Kaisercraft tiny lilac self-
   adhesive rhinestones
Creative Memories Corner
   Maker punch (#610968)

1. Form a 4¼ x 5½-inch card from cardstock. Round bottom corners.

2. Stamp butterfly and sentiment onto card front as shown. Color butterfly with markers.

3. Adhere rhinestones to card as shown. ●

tip

Round corners of base to add interest.

Add depth to a single-layer card using markers to color the focal image.

Thinking of You

Design by Michelle Woerner

tip

Add gem accents in a visual triangle.

Use pen details to pull the design together and lead the eye around the card.

Materials

Gina K. Designs cardstock: white, turquoise sea
Unity Stamp Co. stamp sets: The Simple Things, Flowers + Friends = Priceless
Ink pads: Clearsnap pigment (sapphire silk, curry, robin's egg); Imagine Crafts/Tsukineko Memento (tuxedo black)
Copic® marker: YR24
Black fine-tip pen
Pizzazz Aplenty clear rhinestones: 2mm, 3mm
Sakura glue pen
Tombow liquid glue

1. Form a 5½ x 4¼-inch card from turquoise cardstock.

2. Stamp leaves onto white cardstock as shown using gold, dark blue and light blue inks.

3. Trim cardstock to 5¼ x 4 inches around stamped images as shown. Using fine-tip pen and a ruler, draw border around edges of cardstock panel.

4. Using black ink, stamp sentiment onto panel as shown. Highlight sentiment border using yellow marker.

5. Adhere stamped panel to card front. Embellish card front with rhinestones, attaching them with glue pen. ●

Sending Warm Thoughts

Design by Tami Mayberry

tip

Use a die-cut border in multiple colors with closely related color temperatures.

Materials

Cardstock: Core'dinations (royal, crab grass, aquamarine); Gina K. Designs (white)
Gina K. Designs Simple Snowflakes stamp set
Clearsnap blueberry dye ink pad
⅜-inch-wide blue/white gingham ribbon
Sizzix Paper Rosette Decorative Strip Die (#656931)
Die-cutting machine
SCRAPBOOK ADHESIVES BY 3L™ adhesive runner

1. Form a 5½ x 4¼-inch card from white cardstock.

2. Die-cut 5½-inch-long strips from blue, light green and turquoise cardstock. Trim strips as needed; layer and adhere strips to card front as shown.

3. Adhere ribbon to card front along top edge of layered strips. Tie a bow from ribbon; trim ends at an angle and adhere to card.

4. Stamp sentiment onto card front as shown. ●

With Sympathy

Design by Tami Mayberry

Materials
Gina K. Designs gray cardstock
Gina K. Designs stamp sets: Hello
  Sunshine, All Occasion Tags 2
Clearsnap frost white pigment ink pad
Clearsnap white embossing powder
Want2Scrap gun metal self-
  adhesive pearls
Fiskars corner rounder punch
Embossing heat tool

1. Form a 5½ x 4¼-inch card from cardstock. Round upper right corner.

2. Stamp flowers and sentiment onto card as shown; sprinkle embossing powder over images and heat-emboss.

3. Add pearls to flower centers. ●

tip

Use white ink and embossing powder to add soft and subtle color.

Song in My Heart

Design by Tami Mayberry

Materials
Cardstock: Gina K. Designs (turquoise sea); My Favorite Things (steel gray)
Stamps: guitar, music-theme sentiment
Clearsnap dye ink pads: mermaid, kettle
Want2Scrap gun metal self-adhesive pearls
⅜-inch-wide teal grosgrain ribbon
SCRAPBOOK ADHESIVES BY 3L™: adhesive foam squares, adhesive runner

1. Form a 4¼ x 5½-inch card from gray cardstock.

2. Cut a 4 x 5¼-inch piece from turquoise cardstock. Wrap with ribbon near top as shown, securing with adhesive. Tie ends in a knot, trimming ends at an angle.

3. Using turquoise ink, stamp guitar image onto turquoise cardstock as shown. Stamp sentiment on top of guitar with black ink. Embellish with pearls.

4. Attach panel to card front using foam squares. ●

tip

Stamp a greeting over an image that has been stamped in a monochromatic color.

Miss You

Design by Tami Mayberry

1. Form a 4 x 9-inch card from dark teal cardstock.

2. Cut a 3¾ x 8¾-inch piece from aqua dot cardstock. Cut a 1½ x 8¾-inch strip from teal/white chevron patterned paper; adhere to dot cardstock panel as shown.

3. Die-cut a 2 x 2-inch Lovely Labels shape from dark teal cardstock and a 1½ x 1½-inch Lovely Labels shape from teal/white dot patterned paper. Layer and adhere labels together.

4. Thread ribbon through label slots; adhere ribbon and labels to paper panel as shown, adhering ribbon ends to reverse side. Adhere panel to card front.

5. Stamp sentiment onto ivory cardstock. Die-cut a 1¾ x ⅝-inch oval around sentiment using center of a Lovely Labels shape; adhere to card as shown. ●

Materials

Core'dinations cardstock: Core Essentials (Arctic pool, ivory), Jillian Dot (aqueduct)
Jillibean Soup Soup Staples II Collection Pack patterned paper
The Stamps of Life crayons2stamp stamp set
Clearsnap turquoise pigment ink pad
May Arts ⅜-inch-wide teal grosgrain ribbon
Sizzix Lovely Labels dies (#658051)
Die-cutting machine
SCRAPBOOK ADHESIVES BY 3L™ adhesive runner

Happy Anniversary

Design by Tami Mayberry

tip

Add punched images in various colors.

Place gems in centers of punched shapes to help lead the eye down to the greeting.

Materials
Core'dinations cardstock: Core
   Essentials (fortune teller, Ming,
   celestial, Malaysian orchid),
   Jillian Dot (snowflake)
Core'dinations David Tutera Black/
   White sentiment stickers
Want2Scrap purple self-
   adhesive rhinestones
Martha Stewart 1-inch butterfly punch
Distressing tool
SCRAPBOOK ADHESIVES BY 3L™: adhesive
   foam squares, adhesive runner

1. Form a 4¼ x 5½-inch card from purple cardstock.

2. Cut a 4 x 5¼-inch piece from white dotted cardstock; distress edges and adhere to card front.

3. Punch butterflies from blue-violet, blue and orchid cardstock; attach rhinestones as shown.

4. Attach butterflies and sentiment to card front as shown using foam squares. ●

Life in Your Years

Design by Tami Mayberry

Materials

Cardstock: Core'dinations (French roast, tulip); Gina K. Designs (turquoise sea)
Unity Stamp Co. Moments in Bloom stamp set
Clearsnap ink pads: chalk (chestnut roan), dye (chocolate)
Sizzix Labels, Ornate #2 dies (#658203)
Sizzix Chevrons & Flourishes embossing folder set (#658284)
Die-cutting and embossing machine
SCRAPBOOK ADHESIVES BY 3L™: adhesive foam squares, adhesive runner

1. Form a 4¼ x 5½-inch card from yellow cardstock.

2. Cut a 3⅞ x 5⅛-inch piece from turquoise cardstock; emboss using Flourishes embossing folder. Adhere to brown cardstock and trim, leaving a narrow border. Adhere to card front.

3. Die-cut a 2¾ x 4-inch Ornate Label from turquoise cardstock; center and adhere to card front as shown.

4. Using light brown ink, stamp floral image onto turquoise cardstock. Stamp sentiment on top of floral image using dark brown ink as shown.

5. Die-cut a 2¼ x 3¼-inch Ornate Label around stamped images; ink edges light brown. Attach to card front as shown using foam squares. ●

tip

Ink edges and use dark mats to make layers pop.

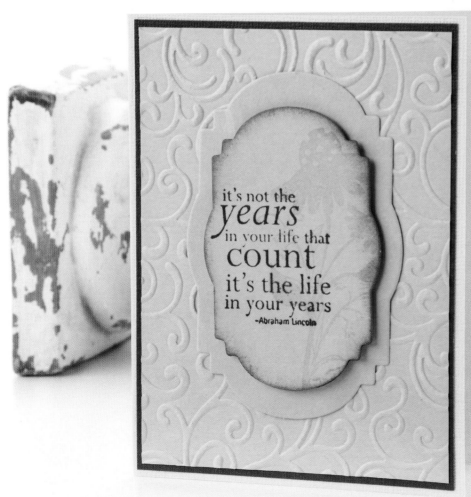

it's not the *years* in your life that **count** it's the life in your years
–Abraham Lincoln

From the Bottom of My Heart

Design by Tami Mayberry

Materials
Gina K. Designs white cardstock
Gina K. Designs Simple Hearts stamp set
Clearsnap kettle dye ink pad
Clearsnap Smooch Spritz
    cherry ice spray ink
Momenta red glitter heart sticker

1. Form a 4¼ x 5½-inch card from cardstock.

2. Spritz card with color spray; let dry.

3. Stamp sentiment onto card as shown; add heart sticker. ●

tip

Add a spritz of color with spray accent inks.

Just a Note

Design by Latisha Yoast

Note the diagonal line created with the knot, greeting and pearls.

Materials
Papertrey Ink kraft cardstock
Clear and Simple All Occasions
    2 stamp set
Imagine Crafts/Tsukineko Memento
    ink pads: tuxedo black, lady bug
Want2Scrap tiny black self-
    adhesive pearls
May Arts ⅝-inch-wide red/ivory
    cotton/stripes ribbon
Creative Memories Corner
    Maker punch (#610968)
Scor-Pal scoring board

1. Form a 4¼ x 5½-inch card from cardstock. Round bottom right corner.

2. On card front, score two parallel vertical lines starting ⅜ inch from left edge; score three parallel horizontal lines starting 1¼ inches from bottom edge. *Note: When scoring, place card front facedown on scoring board to emboss on inside surface of card.*

3. Stamp sentiment three times onto card front using black and red inks as shown.

4. Wrap ribbon around card front, tying ends in a bow and trimming ends at an angle as shown.

5. Adhere pearls just below scored lines as shown. ●

Rhinestone Thanks

Design by Tami Mayberry

Materials

Cardstock: My Favorite Things
   (steel gray); Gina K. Designs
   (cherry red); black
Stamps: decorative background,
   "Thank You"
Clearsnap dye ink pads: kettle, raspberry
Want2Scrap self-adhesive rhinestones:
   black, Nestabling Heart Circles
   1½-inch black rhinestone circle
My Favorite Things ⅝-inch-wide
   steel gray grosgrain ribbon
Sizzix dies: Circles (#657551),
   Mini Hearts (#657212)
Die-cutting machine
SCRAPBOOK ADHESIVES BY 3L™: adhesive
   foam squares, adhesive runner

1. Form a 5½ x 4¼-inch card from gray cardstock.

2. Cut a 5¼ x 4-inch piece from red cardstock. Stamp with background image using red ink.

3. Die-cut a 1⅛-inch circle from black cardstock and a 1⅝-inch circle from gray cardstock; layer and adhere circles together. Attach rhinestone circle to gray circle.

4. Using black ink, stamp sentiment onto red cardstock. Die-cut a 1½-inch heart around sentiment; embellish with rhinestones.

tip

Fill white space with a background stamp in a monochromatic color.

5. Adhere ribbon to stamped red cardstock as shown, wrapping and adhering ribbon ends to back. Adhere circles to cardstock over ribbon; attach heart using a foam square.

6. Attach cardstock panel to card front using foam squares. ●

Get Well Soon

Design by Tami Mayberry

Materials
Core'dinations cardstock: cardinal, scotch, marine blue, nostalgia
Gina K. Designs Ticket Trio stamp set
Dark gray ink pad
Want2Scrap Nestabling Heart Circles 1¼-inch black self-adhesive rhinestone circle
Fiskars corner rounder punch
SCRAPBOOK ADHESIVES BY 3L™ adhesive runner

1. Form a 4½ x 4½-inch card from gray cardstock. Round right-hand corners.

2. Stamp ticket images onto red, yellow and blue cardstocks; stamp sentiment onto yellow ticket. Cut out tickets and adhere to card front as shown.

3. Attach rhinestone circle to card as shown. ●

Accent a greeting with blocks of color.

Snowflake Trio

Design by Laura Williams

Materials
DiscountCardstock.com cardstock:
    brilliant white, midnight black
Gina K. Designs Simple
    Snowflake stamp set
Close To My Heart archival black ink pad
Close To My Heart 1⅛-inch-wide
    black striped grosgrain ribbon
Uchida Clever Lever Jumbo
    1-inch circle punch
EK Success adhesive foam dots
Scor-Pal ¼-inch-wide double-
    sided adhesive

1. Form a 4¼ x 5½-inch card from white cardstock.

2. Cut a 2 x 4¼-inch piece from white cardstock. Stamp 1½-inch snowflakes onto ends of panel as shown.

3. Adhere stamped panel to black cardstock and trim, leaving a small border. Adhere panel to card front as shown.

4. Stamp a 1-inch snowflake onto a scrap of white cardstock; punch a circle around snowflake and attach to card front as shown using foam dot.

5. Tie ribbon in a bow; trim ends at an angle. Adhere bow to card as shown. ●

tip

Use black-and-white images for a dramatic effect.

Note the vertical line created by the bow and circle images.

Hugs

Design by Tami Mayberry

tip

Add color with a two-step stamping process.

Materials

Gina K. Designs cardstock: red hot, white
Gina K. Designs Simple Hearts stamp set
Clearsnap dye ink pads: strawberry, kettle
Want2Scrap silver self-adhesive rhinestones
Gina K. Designs ⅝-inch-wide red/white stitched grosgrain ribbon
Sizzix Circles, Scallop dies (#657552)
Die-cutting machine
SCRAPBOOK ADHESIVES BY 3L™: adhesive foam squares, adhesive runner

1. Form a 4½ x 5⅝-inch card from white cardstock.

2. Cut a 4¼ x 5⅜-inch piece from white cardstock. Adhere to red cardstock and trim, leaving a very narrow border.

3. Wrap layered cardstock panel with ribbon as shown; adhere panel to card front.

4. Using black ink, stamp sentiment onto card front as shown. Using black ink, stamp image onto a piece of white cardstock; stamp solid hearts inside heart outlines with red ink to fill in.

5. Die-cut a 2-inch scalloped circle around stamped image; embellish hearts with rhinestones. Attach stamped circle to card as shown using foam squares. ●

It's Your Day

Design by Tami Mayberry

Materials
Core'dinations cardstock: grassroots, crab grass, Bermuda
Jillibean Soup Birthday Soup Labels stickers
Want2Scrap turquoise self-adhesive rhinestones
May Arts ½-inch-wide turquoise/green sheer stripes ribbon
⅞-inch star punch
SCRAPBOOK ADHESIVES BY 3L™: adhesive foam squares, adhesive runner

1. Form a 4¼ x 5½-inch card from teal cardstock.

2. Cut a 4 x 5¼-inch piece from light green cardstock. Wrap ribbon around green panel and tie ends into a bow as shown; trim ends at an angle.

3. Punch a star from dark green cardstock; attach to bow using foam square. Adhere birthday label sticker to panel as shown, trimming edge as needed. Embellish star and label with rhinestones.

4. Attach panel to card front using foam squares. ●

Use your favorite ribbon as inspiration for the color palette for a card.

Happy Birthday to You

Design by Tami Mayberry

happy birthday to you ◉ happy birthday to you ◉ happy birthday to you

Materials
Core'dinations cardstock:
   nightfall, snowflake
Stickers: SRM Stickers (We've Got
   Your Border Birthday); Momenta
   (Kaleidoscope Mini Puffy Dot)
SCRAPBOOK ADHESIVES BY 3L™
   adhesive runner

1. Form a 9 x 4-inch card from black cardstock.

2. Cut an 8¾ x 3¾-inch piece from white cardstock. Adhere birthday stickers to cardstock panel as shown; adhere puffy stickers between phrases.

3. Center and adhere panel to card front. ●

tip

Use brightly colored stickers to add color to a black-and-white card.

ConGRADulations

Design by Laura Williams

Materials
DiscountCardstock.com
    brilliant white cardstock
Paper Smooches Smarty Pants stamp set
Close To My Heart archival black ink pad
ShinHan Touch Twin markers:
    7, 25, 35, CG1

1. Form a 4 x 5½-inch card from cardstock.

2. Stamp pencils and sentiment onto card as shown.

3. Color pencils with markers. ●

tip

Create a border of repeated stamped images and color with markers.

Too Much Happy

Design by Tami Mayberry

tip

Use patterned papers as both a decorative border and a greeting.

Score and sand vertical lines along border to draw the eyes downward.

Materials

Core'dinations navy cardstock
Simple Stories Summer Fresh
   6 x 6 paper pad
Want2Scrap silver self-
   adhesive rhinestones
Fiskars corner rounder punch
Scor-Pal scoring board
Sandpaper
SCRAPBOOK ADHESIVES BY 3L™
   adhesive runner

1. Form a 4¼ x 5½-inch card from cardstock. Round upper right corner.

2. Score a vertical line down card front near fold; score another line 1¾ inches from the first. *Note: When scoring, place card front facedown on scoring board to emboss on inside surface of card.* Lightly sand scored lines on card front.

3. Cut a 1 x 5½-inch strip with sentiment from patterned paper; adhere paper to a 1½ x 5½-inch strip of green dot paper. Adhere to card front between scored lines.

4. Embellish patterned paper with rhinestones. ●

Hello

Design by Tami Mayberry

tip

Emboss multicolored blocks with the same pattern, rotating the pattern for variety.

The rotated design on the embossing leads the eye in a circular pattern around the card.

Materials

Core'dinations cardstock: Core Essentials (roasted pepper, sutter butter, marsh, beach, fern), Tim Holtz Kraft-Core (No. 22)
Simple Stories Sn@p! Stickers Icons sticker sheet
Want2Scrap amber self-adhesive rhinestones
Sizzix Chevrons & Flourishes embossing folder set (#658284)
Die-cutting and embossing machine
SCRAPBOOK ADHESIVES BY 3L™: adhesive foam squares, adhesive runner

1. Form a 4¼ x 4¼-inch card from kraft cardstock.

2. Cut a 4 x 4-inch piece from light tan cardstock; center and attach to card front using foam squares.

3. Cut four 1½ x 1½-inch pieces, one each from green, red, yellow and blue cardstock; emboss with Chevrons embossing folder. Adhere to card front as shown.

4. Attach sticker using foam square. Embellish card with rhinestones. ●

Deepest Sympathy

Design by Tami Mayberry

Materials
Core'dinations Vienna lake cardstock
Core'dinations David Tutera Sympathy
    Sentiments embellishment
Sizzix Squares, Scallop dies (#657566)
Sizzix Ornate Frame & Borders
    embossing folder set (#658216)
Sizzix Big Shot die-cutting and
    embossing machine

1. Form a 4¼ x 4¼-inch card from cardstock.

2. Position card just below top edge of 4⅛ x 4⅛-inch Square, Scallop die to preserve top fold; die-cut card.

3. Emboss card front using Swirls embossing folder as shown.

4. Attach premade sentiment embellishment. ●

tip

Use embossing, textured cardstock and scalloped edges to dress up premade embellishments.

Birthday Wishes

Design by Latisha Yoast

Materials

Bazzill Basics cardstock: yellow, white
October Afternoon Midway
    8 x 8 paper pad
Waltzingmouse Stamps Say
    It Loud stamp set
Imagine Crafts/Tsukineko Memento
    tuxedo black ink pad
Lawn Fawn Trimmings
    goldenrod hemp cord
SCRAPBOOK ADHESIVES BY 3L™
    adhesive foam squares

1. Form a 9 x 4-inch card from yellow cardstock.

2. Cut an 8¾ x 3¾-inch piece from white cardstock; stamp sentiment onto cardstock as shown.

3. Cut a 1 x 3-inch piece and a 1 x 1¾-inch piece from patterned paper; cut a V-notch in one end of each piece. Attach pieces to cardstock as shown.

Use typography in various sizes to draw interest to a focal-point greeting.

4. Wrap cord around cardstock panel as shown, tying ends in a bow.

5. Attach cardstock panel to card front. ●

Simple Greetings

Design by Tami Mayberry

tip

Use designs preprinted onto patterned papers as the focal image.

Materials

Core'dinations cardstock: Tim Holtz Kraft-Core (No. 6), Core Essentials (red pepper)
My Mind's Eye The Sweetest Thing Tangerine 6 x 6 paper pad
Simple Stories Sn@p! Typeset letter stickers
Want2Scrap yellow self-adhesive rhinestones
SCRAPBOOK ADHESIVES BY 3L™ adhesive runner

1. Form a 4½ x 6¼-inch card from gold cardstock.

2. Cut a 4 x 5¾-inch piece from patterned paper; adhere to red-orange cardstock and trim, leaving a small border. Adhere panel to card front.

3. Attach stickers to spell sentiment; embellish flowers with rhinestones. ●

Pack a Bag

Design by Jeanne Streiff

tip

Layer a patterned image with a 3-D panel to extend the pattern.

Materials

DiscountCardstock.com brilliant white cardstock
The Paper Loft Everyday Life Head in the Clouds patterned paper
The Paper Loft Everyday Life Vacation cardstock stickers
Clearsnap chocolate dye ink pad
Blue button
The Twinery denim baker's twine
Sponge
SCRAPBOOK ADHESIVES BY 3L™: adhesive foam squares, adhesive strips

1. Form a 4¼ x 5½-inch card from cardstock.

2. Cut a 4⅛ x 5⅜-inch piece from patterned paper, centering balloon; ink edges. Adhere paper to card front.

3. Cut a 3½ x 4¾-inch piece from cardstock.

4. Cut a 3⅜ x 4⅝-inch piece from patterned paper, centering balloon; ink edges. Adhere paper to white cardstock; attach to card front as shown using foam squares.

5. Ink edges of sentiment sticker; adhere to card front as shown. Thread button onto twine; tie twine into a bow. Attach button to card as shown using a foam square. ●

Life Is a Dream

Design by Jeanne Streiff

Materials

DiscountCardstock.com cardstock: Prussian blue, brilliant white
Unity Stamp Co. Birdie Inspiration stamp set
Clearsnap chalk ink pads: chestnut roan, Prussian blue
Sponge
SCRAPBOOK ADHESIVES BY 3L™ adhesive foam squares

1. Form a 4¼ x 4¼-inch card from blue cardstock.

2. Using brown ink, stamp stem buds along edge of card front to create border; stamp sentiment onto card as shown. Stamp flourish onto card front as shown with blue ink.

3. Using blue ink, stamp cloud shape onto white cardstock; stamp flourish off edge as shown. Cut out shape; sponge edges brown. Using foam squares, attach cloud to card front, aligning stamped flourishes.

4. Stamp bird onto white cardstock with brown ink. Sponge bird's lower body and wings brown; sponge tail and back blue. Cut out and attach bird to cloud as shown using foam squares. ●

tip

Stamp a focal image onto both a panel and a base image.

Draw interest to the focal image by sponging edges.

You Rock!

Design by Stephanie Washburn

The bright pink ribbon on this card leads the eye across the card, drawing attention to the greeting.

Materials
Papertrey Ink white cardstock
Simple Stories Sn@p! Basics
   6 x 6 paper pad
Simple Stories 3 x 4 Sn@p!
   Cards Snappy Sayings
Alphabet stamp set
Ranger Distress walnut stain ink pad
Papertrey Ink ⅜-inch-wide raspberry
   fizz twill tape ribbon
Adhesive foam dots
Scor-Pal ¼-inch-wide double-
   sided adhesive

1. Form a 4¼ x 5½-inch card from white cardstock. Cut a 4¼ x 5½-inch piece from patterned paper; adhere to card front.

2. Cut a 3¼ x 4-inch piece from white cardstock. Trim a 3 x 4-inch Snappy Sayings card to 3 x 3 inches and adhere to cardstock piece as shown. Stamp sentiment onto bottom of cardstock panel.

3. Wrap a 4-inch length of ribbon around panel as shown, adhering ends to back. Tie another length of ribbon into a bow; trim ends. Adhere bow to panel as shown. Attach panel to card front using foam dots. ●

Fluttery Butterflies

Design by Tami Mayberry

Materials

Core'dinations Tillie Dot cardstock:
    mantis, love potion
Core'dinations premade A6 card
Stickers: SRM Stickers (Fancy Sentiments
    Thinking of You); Momenta (3D
    Kaleidoscope butterflies, flower)
May Arts ½-inch-wide fuchsia
    solid wrinkled ribbon
Corner rounder punch
SCRAPBOOK ADHESIVES BY 3L™
    adhesive runner

1. Round upper right corner of card.

2. Cut a 4¼ x 6-inch piece from light green embossed cardstock and a 2 x 6-inch piece from fuchsia embossed cardstock. Layer and adhere fuchsia cardstock onto light green cardstock with right edges even; round upper right corner.

3. Wrap ribbon around cardstock panel, tying ends into a bow as shown. Center and adhere panel to card front.

4. Embellish card with stickers. ●

tip

Create a background from multiple colors of the same pre-embossed cardstock design.

Happy Days

Design by Kimberly Crawford

Materials
Bazzill Basics kraft cardstock
My Mind's Eye patterned papers: Miss
    Caroline Fiddlesticks 6 x 6 paper pad,
    Dolled Up Day Butterflies 12 x 12 sheet
Complementary buttons
SCRAPBOOK ADHESIVES BY 3L™:
    adhesive foam squares, adhesive
    dots, adhesive runner

1. Form a 4¼ x 5½-inch card from cardstock.

2. Cut a slightly smaller piece from Fiddlesticks woodgrain paper; adhere to card front.

3. Cut butterflies from Butterflies paper; cut sentiment from Fiddlesticks Journaling Card. Attach to card front as shown using foam squares.

4. Attach buttons to butterflies using adhesive dots. ●

tip

Use patterned paper not only to create a simple background design but also to help draw the eye to the sentiment.

Lucky Stars

Design by Jeanne Streiff

Materials

Bazzill Basics Simply Smooth
ivory cardstock
The Paper Loft blue/yellow
patterned paper
Hero Arts Year Round
Sentiments stamp set
Clearsnap dye ink pads:
licorice, cornflower
Sakura black fine-tip pen
Blue self-adhesive gems
EK Success large corner rounder punch
3M adhesives: adhesive foam
tape, adhesive runner

1. Form a 4¼ x 5½-inch card from cardstock; round upper corners.

2. Cut a 4 x 3¾-inch piece from yellow patterned paper; round corrners. Stamp sentiment onto paper as shown using black ink. Randomly stamp small stars onto paper with blue ink. Outline rectangle with pen.

3. Cut a 1⅜ x 5½-inch piece from blue patterned paper. Stamp 1¼-inch stars onto paper as shown using blue ink; outline long edges of strip with pen.

Add repeated images in varying sizes. Use patterns that accent the greeting theme.

4. Using blue ink, stamp two stars onto yellow patterned paper; cut out. Attach stars to stamped strip as shown using foam tape.

5. Adhere stamped rectangle and strip to card front as shown. Embellish stars with rhinestones. ●

Hi

Design by Laura Williams

Cut border and background stamped images into squares and mat with solid color.

Materials

DiscountCardstock.com cardstock:
   brilliant white, sea blue smooth
Paper Smooches stamp sets:
   Potpourri, Hang Ups
Clearsnap dye ink pads: banana, licorice
EK Success adhesive foam dots
Close To My Heart glue

1. Form a 4¼ x 6¼-inch card from white cardstock.

2. Using yellow ink, stamp diamond-patterned square image three times onto white cardstock. Cut out squares.

3. Using black ink, stamp sentiment onto one stamped square.

4. Adhere stamped squares to blue cardstock; trim, leaving narrow borders.

5. Attach squares to card front as shown using foam dots. ●

For My Friend

Design by Tami Mayberry

The flourish-style embossing of the border ties in the base design with the butterfly in the greeting.

1. Form a 5½ x 4¼-inch card from dark red cardstock.

2. Cut a 5 x 3¾-inch piece from teal cardstock. Emboss as shown using Flourish embossing folder; lightly sand embossed design.

3. Adhere embossed cardstock to gold cardstock and trim, leaving a small border. Adhere panel to card front.

4. Stamp polka-dot tag image twice, once on dark red cardstock and once on gold cardstock. Stamp sentiment onto center of gold tag.

tip

Use embossing and sandable cardstock to add border patterns.

5. Die-cut a 2⅞ x 1⅜-inch Grommet Tags shape around tag image on dark red cardstock. Cut out center section from tag image on gold cardstock; attach to dark red tag using foam squares.

6. Attach layered tag to card front using foam squares and attach rhinestones as shown. ●

Feel the Joy

Design by Tami Mayberry

Materials

Core'dinations cardstock:
  marsh, rustic, fern
Simple Stories Happy Day 6 x 6 paper pad
Unity Stamp Co. Feel the Joy stamp set
Clearsnap kettle dye ink pad
Green self-adhesive pearl
May Arts ½-inch-wide olive
  solid wrinkled ribbon
SCRAPBOOK ADHESIVES BY 3L™: adhesive
  foam squares, adhesive runner

1. Form a 4½ x 6¼-inch card from green cardstock.

2. Cut a 3¾ x 5-inch piece from patterned paper. Stamp image and sentiment onto paper as shown.

3. Adhere stamped paper to teal cardstock and trim, leaving a small border. Wrap panel with ribbon as shown, tying ends in a bow; secure ribbon with adhesive. Attach pearl to bow center.

4. Adhere panel to rust cardstock and trim, leaving a small border. Attach panel to card front using foam squares. ●

tip

Stamp images onto patterned paper.

Forever Friends

Design by Tami Mayberry

tip

Use the same pattern in multiple colors to provide continuity.

Materials

Core'dinations Whitewash grandma's rocker cardstock
Jillibean Soup Soup Staples II 12 x 12 patterned paper pack
The Stamps of Life Search4Words stamp set
Clearsnap kettle dye ink pad
Want2Scrap self-adhesive rhinestones: light blue, orange, light green
Scor-Pal scoring board
Sandpaper
SCRAPBOOK ADHESIVES BY 3L™ adhesive runner

1. Form a 5½ x 4¼-inch card from cardstock.

2. Beginning ¼ inch from bottom edge, score four horizontal lines, 1 inch apart, across card front. *Note: When scoring, place card front facedown on scoring board to emboss on inside surface of card.* Lightly sand scored lines on card front.

3. Cut three 5½ x ¾-inch strips, one each from turquoise, orange and green patterned papers. Adhere strips to card front between scored lines as shown.

4. Stamp sentiment onto orange strip. Attach rhinestones to matching strips as shown. ●

Rainbow Hello

Design by Stephanie Washburn

Materials

Papertrey Ink white cardstock
Stamps: decorative background, alphabet
A Muse Studio ink pads: blackberry, cherry, cobalt, grass, orange, slate
We R Memory Keepers Crop-A-Dile Corner Chomper
3M adhesive foam tape

1. Form a 4¼ x 5½-inch card from cardstock.

2. Using gray ink, stamp surface with background stamp.

3. Cut a 3 x 4½-inch piece from cardstock; round off corners. Stamp "HELLO" onto cardstock as shown using purple, blue, green, orange and red inks.

4. Center and attach stamped panel to card front using foam tape. ●

Stamp background with a neutral-color background stamp to add interest to white space.

Repeat one large element in a variety of colors.

Congratulations

Design by Michelle Woerner

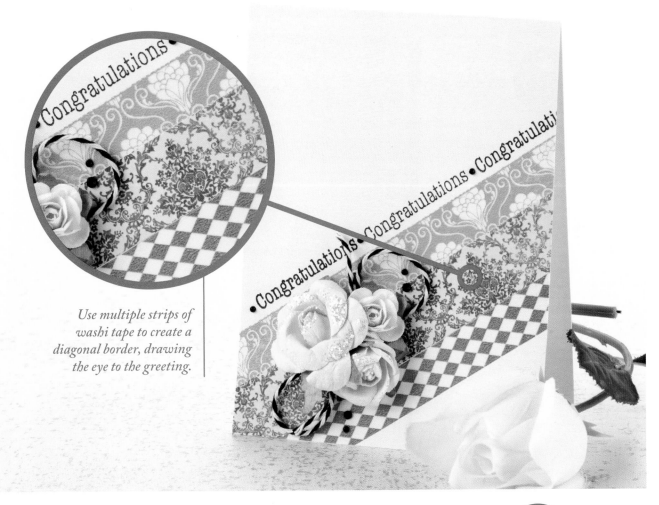

Use multiple strips of washi tape to create a diagonal border, drawing the eye to the greeting.

Materials

Gina K. Designs white cardstock
My Mind's Eye The Sweetest Thing Honey 6 x 6 paper pad
Prima Marketing washi tape: Welcome to Paris, Zephyr
JustRite Papercraft With Gratitude Antique Labels One stamp set
Imagine Crafts/Tsukineko VersaFine black onyx ink pad
Pizzazz Aplenty tiny black rhinestones
Prima Marketing flowers: Interlude C (yellow), Fairytale Roses (white)
The Twinery charcoal baker's twine
Sakura glue pen
Tombow liquid glue

1. Form a 4¼ x 5½-inch card from cardstock.

2. Cut a ⅞ x 7-inch strip of patterned paper; adhere diagonally to card front as shown, trimming edges even. Add strips of washi tape to card as shown, trimming edges.

3. Stamp sentiment onto card front as shown.

4. Tie a 3-inch bow from baker's twine and adhere to lower left corner of card with liquid glue.

tip

When mailing dimensional cards, package them in a padded envelope or a small box.

Arrange flowers over bow as shown; attach with liquid glue.

5. Attach rhinestones as desired using glue pen. ●

A Birthday Note

Design by Tami Mayberry

Materials

Gina K. Designs cardstock: red, white
Jillibean Soup Soup Staples II patterned
    papers: Orange Salt, Yellow
    Salt, Red Salt, Turquoise Salt
SRM Stickers We've Got Your
    Border Birthday stickers
The Twinery maraschino baker's twine
Sizzix Circles dies (#657551)
Die-cutting machine
Sewing machine with turquoise thread
SCRAPBOOK ADHESIVES BY 3L™
    adhesive runner

happy birthday to you

1. Form a 4¼ x 5½-inch card from red cardstock.

2. Cut a 4 x 5¼-inch piece from white cardstock.

3. Die-cut four 1-inch circles from patterned papers. Layer onto white cardstock. Randomly machine-stitch circles in place as shown. Center and adhere cardstock panel to card front.

4. Wrap twine around top of card front, tying ends into a bow. Attach sentiment sticker to card along bottom edge. ●

Thank You

Design by Tami Mayberry

Materials

Cardstock: Core'dinations Vintage
  Collection (Oxford, ruby, autumn);
  Gina K. Designs (white)
Gina K. Designs Masculine Tags stamp set
Clearsnap kettle dye ink pad
⅜-inch-wide teal grosgrain ribbon
Spellbinders™ die templates:
  Hexagons (#S4-368), Nested
  Lacey Pennants (#S5-029)
Sizzix Chevrons & Flourishes
  embossing folder set (#658284)
Die-cutting and embossing machine
SCRAPBOOK ADHESIVES BY 3L™: adhesive
  foam squares, adhesive runner

1. Form a 4¼ x 5½-inch card from teal cardstock.

2. Cut a 4 x 5¼-inch piece from white cardstock. Emboss bottom half as shown using Chevrons embossing folder.

3. Die-cut three ⅞ x ¾-inch Hexagons, one each from teal, dark red and gold cardstock. Cut off ⅛ inch from width of each hexagon. Adhere to embossed cardstock as shown.

4. Wrap ribbon around cardstock panel and tie ends into a bow as shown; trim ribbon ends at an angle. Secure with adhesive as needed.

5. Stamp sentiment onto white cardstock. Die-cut a 3 x ⅜-inch Lacey Pennants ribbon around sentiment; trim length down to 2½ inches. Adhere ribbon to embossed panel as shown.

6. Attach panel to card front using foam squares. ●

tip

Use an embossing folder to partially emboss a panel.

THANK YOU

Welcome Ba-Bee

Design by Latisha Yoast

Note the use of red baker's twine to lead the eye from the large bow downward to the greeting.

Materials
Gina K. Designs white cardstock
Darcie's LLC Where My
    Honey Is stamp set
Imagine Crafts/Tsukineko Memento
    tuxedo black ink pad
Kaisercraft teal self-adhesive rhinestones
May Arts ¾-inch-wide turquoise/
    white twill/chevron stripes ribbon
Lawn Fawn peppermint baker's twine
Spellbinders™ Framed Tags One
    die templates (#S4-392)
Spellbinders™ So Trendy
    embossing folder (#ES-006)
Die-cutting and embossing machine
SCRAPBOOK ADHESIVES BY 3L™
    adhesive foam squares

1. Form a 4¼ x 5½-inch card from cardstock.

2. Cut a 4 x 5¼-inch piece from cardstock; emboss with embossing folder. Wrap ribbon around panel as shown; tie ends into a bow. Center and attach panel to card front with foam squares.

3. Die-cut and emboss a 2⅜ x 1⅜-inch Rectangle Tag from cardstock; stamp with sentiment and embellish with rhinestones.

4. Tie tag to ribbon with twine as shown; secure tag to card front with foam squares. ●

Add interest to a simple white background with an embossed panel that sets off a smooth die-cut tag.

Thanks a Latte

Design by AJ Otto

Materials

Cardstock: Neenah (white); Stampin'
  Up! (soft suede, Baja breeze)
Gina K. Designs Cool Beans stamp set
Clearsnap wicked black dye ink pad
Copic® markers: C00, E35, G0000
Spellbinders™ Standard Circles
  SM dies (#S4-116)
Spellbinders™ Industrial embossing
  folder set (#EL-017)
Spellbinders™ Grand Calibur® with
  Raspberry Spacer Plate (#GC-008)
SCRAPBOOK ADHESIVES BY 3L™
  adhesive foam squares

1. Form a 4¼ x 4¼-inch card from brown cardstock.

2. Cut a 2⅛ x 3¼-inch piece from light blue cardstock; trim upper corners diagonally to form a tag. Stamp sentiment onto tag as shown.

3. Emboss tag using Industrial embossing folder and spacer plate. Attach tag to card front using foam squares.

4. Die-cut and emboss a 2⅛-inch Standard Circle SM shape from white cardstock. Stamp image onto circle; color with markers. Attach circle to card front as shown using foam squares. ●

Add texture to a tag or embellishment to accent the focal point.

Get Well Wishes

Design by Tami Mayberry

tip

Use premade die-cut panels to add texture.

Materials

Core'dinations amaryllis cardstock
Core'dinations David Tutera
    pink A2 Lace Floral Layer
Core'dinations David Tutera
    Sympathy Sentiments stickers
Want2Scrap Nestabling 2⅛-inch
    pink self-adhesive pearl circle
Want2Scrap pink self-
    adhesive rhinestone
SCRAPBOOK ADHESIVES BY 3L™
    adhesive dots

1. Form a 4¼ x 5½-inch card from cardstock.

2. Adhere Lace Floral Layer to card front.

3. Attach "get well soon" sticker to center of card front. Attach pink pearl circle around sticker as shown. Embellish with rhinestone. ●

Hello Sunshine

Design by Laura Williams

tip

Use foam adhesives to add dimension to simple stamped images.

Materials

DiscountCardstock.com cardstock: brilliant white smooth, goldenrod smooth, blue Cascata felt
Gina K. Designs Hello Sunshine stamp set
Clearsnap licorice dye ink pad
EK Success adhesive foam dots
Close To My Heart glue

1. Form a 4¼ x 5½-inch card from white cardstock.

2. Cut a 3 x 4¼-inch piece from blue cardstock; adhere to white cardstock and trim, leaving a very narrow border. Adhere to yellow cardstock and trim, leaving a border. Adhere panel to card front.

3. Stamp two clouds onto white cardstock and a sun onto yellow cardstock. Cut out; adhere sun and one cloud to card front as shown; attach remaining cloud using foam dot.

4. Stamp sentiment onto card front as shown. ●

Thanks So Much

Design by Tami Mayberry

Materials
Core'dinations cardstock:
  Vintage Collection (Oxford),
  Core Essentials (scarlet)
Gina K. Designs All Occasion
  Tags stamp set
Clearsnap raspberry dye ink pad
Want2Scrap light blue self-
  adhesive gems
Spellbinders™ Grommet Tags
  die templates (#S4-322)
Sizzix Snowflake & Flourish
  embossing folder set (#656973)
Die-cutting and embossing machine
Core'dinations sanding block
Core'dinations Dust Buddy
SCRAPBOOK ADHESIVES BY 3L™: adhesive
  foam squares, adhesive runner

1. Form a 4¼ x 4¼-inch card from teal cardstock.

2. Cut a 4 x 4-inch piece from red cardstock. Emboss as shown using Flourish embossing folder; lightly sand embossed design. Adhere embossed cardstock to card front.

3. Stamp tag image twice, once onto red cardstock and once onto smooth side of teal cardstock. Stamp sentiment onto center of teal tag.

4. Die-cut a 2⅞ x 1⅜-inch Grommet Tags shape around tag

Cut out stamped images and layer onto a panel to add dimension.

image on red cardstock. Cut out center section from tag image on teal cardstock; adhere to red tag using foam squares.

5. Adhere layered tag to card front and attach rhinestones as shown. ●

So Sweet

Design by Laura Williams

A visual triangle of embellishments and horizontal lines of the patterned paper draws the eye to the greeting.

Materials

DiscountCardstock.com
   cardstock: kraft, brown
Simple Stories Fab-U-lous Collection
   100% Girl patterned paper
Simple Stories Fab-U-lous 12 x 12
   Fundamentals cardstock stickers
Want2Scrap pink self-adhesive pearls
EK Success adhesive foam dots
Close To My Heart glue pen

1. Form a 5½ x 4¼-inch card from kraft cardstock.

2. Cut a 3¼ x 2¼-inch piece from patterned paper; adhere to brown cardstock and trim, leaving a small border. Center and adhere to card front.

3. Adhere sentiment sticker to kraft cardstock and trim, leaving a small border. Layer onto brown cardstock and trim, leaving a small border. Attach sentiment to card as shown using foam dots.

Use foam adhesive with premade embellishments such as stickers to add dimension.

4. Adhere flower sticker and butterfly stickers as shown, using foam dots to attach butterflies. Embellish butterflies with pearls. ●

Birthday Greetings

Design by Jeanne Streiff

tip

Add texture with lace and trims.

Materials

DiscountCardstock.com cardstock:
  chili smooth, brilliant white
Hero Arts stamp sets: Find Joy,
  Sew Me Flower Jewel
Clearsnap ink pads: chalk (berrylicious),
  dye (licorice, chocolate)
ShinHan Art Touch Twin markers:
  P82, P85, RP87, YG48
Flower Soft® ivory color sprinkles
May Arts 1½-inch-wide ivory crochet trim
Sizzix Frames with Sprigs die
  and stamp set (#657775)
Sizzix Big Shot die-cutting and
  embossing machine
Sponge
Flower Soft® glue
SCRAPBOOK ADHESIVES BY 3L™:
  adhesive foam squares, permanent
  adhesive strips

1. Form a 4¼ x 5½-inch card from burgundy cardstock.

2. Cut a 4 x 5¼-inch piece from white cardstock; sponge edges berry. Wrap crochet trim around cardstock panel as shown; center and adhere panel to card front.

3. Stamp frame onto white cardstock using berry ink; color with markers. Die-cut a 3½ x 1⅝-inch label around image; sponge edges brown. Attach to card front as shown using foam squares.

4. Stamp flower onto white cardstock using black ink; color

with markers. Cut out; attach to card front as shown using foam square.

5. Embellish flower center and flower centers on label using glue and color sprinkles.

6. Stamp sentiment onto white cardstock using black ink. Cut a 3 x ⅝-inch rectangle around sentiment; V-notch one end. Sponge edges brown. Adhere to burgundy cardstock; trim, leaving narrow borders along long edges. Attach to card front as shown using foam squares. ●

Dig You

Design by Tami Mayberry

1. Form a 4¼ x 5½-inch card from gold cardstock. Die-cut a 2½-inch square opening in card front ½ inch from top edge.

2. Using black ink, stamp image onto white cardstock; color with markers. Die-cut a 2-inch square around stamped image.

3. Die-cut a 2½-inch square from brown cardstock. Center and attach stamped image to brown square using foam squares. Adhere matted image inside card, positioning it inside window opening.

4. Embellish card front with rhinestones. Using brown ink, stamp sentiment inside card. ●

Materials

Cardstock: Gina K. Designs (white); Core'dinations (Core Essentials brownie, Vintage Collection autumn)
Unity Stamp Co. I Dig You stamp set
Clearsnap dye ink pads: kettle, chocolate
ShinHan Art Touch Twin markers: B65, BR102, CG1, CG7, R11
Want2Scrap turquoise self-adhesive rhinestones
Sizzix Squares dies (#657565)
Die-cutting machine
SCRAPBOOK ADHESIVES BY 3L™: adhesive foam squares, adhesive runner

tip

Add a die-cut window to a card instead of placing all the elements on the card front.

Inside of card

Always on My Mind

Design by Laura Williams

tip

Create an elegant texture with shimmery cardstock, sheer ribbon and heat embossing.

Materials

DiscountCardstock.com: brilliant
    white, blue steel metallic
Gina K. Designs Hello Sunshine stamp set
Close To My Heart embossing ink pad
Clearsnap pearl embossing powder
Offray ½-inch-wide white
    organdy ribbon
Embossing heat tool
EK Success adhesive foam squares
Close To My Heart glue pen

1. Form a 4¼ x 5½-inch card from dark blue cardstock.

2. Cut a 3 x 4¼-inch piece from dark blue cardstock. Stamp image and sentiment onto cardstock as shown; sprinkle embossing powder over images and heat-emboss.

3. Wrap ribbon around embossed cardstock as shown, tying ends in a bow.

4. Adhere cardstock panel to white cardstock and trim, leaving a very narrow border. Center and attach panel to card front with foam squares. ●

LOVE

Design by Tami Mayberry

Materials

Core'dinations cardstock: Core Essentials (Mediterranean), Gemstone (yellow topaz, moonstone)
Momenta stickers: Flutter/Glitter Clear Layered butterfly, Family Ties/Male Puffy Message "Love"
Sizzix Chevrons & Flourishes embossing folder set (#658284)
Die-cutting and embossing machine
SCRAPBOOK ADHESIVES BY 3L™ adhesive runner

1. Form a 5½ x 4¼-inch card from dark blue cardstock.

2. Cut a 5 x 3¾-inch piece from light blue cardstock; adhere to gold cardstock and trim, leaving a narrow border. Center and adhere to card front.

3. Cut a 5 x 1¾-inch piece from gold cardstock. Emboss with Flourishes embossing folder; adhere to card front as shown.

4. Adhere butterfly and sentiment stickers. ●

Use 3-D embellishments and embossing to add texture and dimension.

Happy Birthday

Design by Tami Mayberry

Materials

Cardstock: Gina K. Designs (white); Core'dinations (stormy gray)
American Crafts Happy Birthday Set 1 stickers
American Crafts Chap Elements striped brad
Want2Scrap white self-adhesive pearls
May Arts ½-inch-wide white sheer/satin band ribbon
Sizzix dies: Labels, Ornate #3 (#658204), Ovals (#657563), Tattered Florals (#656640)
Sizzix embossing folders: Ornate Frames Set #2 (#658215), Flower Rings & Clusters Set (#657255)
Die-cutting and embossing machine
Paper piercing tool
SCRAPBOOK ADHESIVES BY 3L™: adhesive foam squares, adhesive runner

1. Form a 5½ x 4¼-inch card from gray cardstock.

2. Cut a 5¼ x 4-inch piece from white cardstock; emboss with polka-dot Ornate Frames embossing folder.

3. Emboss another piece of white cardstock with Flower Rings embossing folder; die-cut a 3⅞ x 2⅜-inch Ornate Labels shape from embossed cardstock. Center and adhere to embossed frame.

4. Wrap ribbon around cardstock panel, tying ends in a bow as shown. Attach panel to card front using foam squares.

5. Die-cut a 1-inch Tattered Florals flower from white cardstock. Pierce a hole through flower center; attach brad. Adhere flower to ribbon bow as shown.

6. Die-cut a 2 x ⅝-inch oval from white cardstock; adhere sentiment sticker to oval. Attach oval to card front as shown using foam squares.

7. Embellish card front with pearls. ●

tip

Add interest with multiple embossed patterns and embellishments in the same color.

The horizontal lines of the ribbon edges and brad pattern draw the eye across the card to the greeting.

Thanks

Design by Debby Hughes

tip

Layer multiple die-cut images to build a scene.

Materials
Craftwork Cards white cardstock
Lawn Fawn Dewey Decimal Petite
    patterned paper pack
Dies: Lil' Inker Designs (Stitched
    Mats: Rectangles); Memory Box
    (Country Landscape #98239,
    Script Thanks #98240)
Die-cutting machine
Ranger Glossy Accents adhesive
Stampin' Up! adhesive foam dots

1. Form a 4 x 5½-inch card from cardstock.

2. Die-cut a 3 x 4¼-inch Stitched Rectangle from patterned paper.

3. Die-cut a piece of white cardstock using Country Landscape die; die-cut again using 3 x 4¼-inch Stitched Rectangles die, forming a 3 x 2½-inch piece as shown. Using foam dots, attach die-cut cardstock to patterned paper panel with bottom edges even.

4. Die-cut and emboss a 4 x 1⅛-inch "thanks" from contrasting patterned paper; adhere to panel as shown. Using foam dots, attach panel to card front. ●

Dream, Create, Inspire

Design by Jeanne Streiff

1. Form a 4¼ x 5½-inch card from tan cardstock. Round upper corners. Ink edges brown.

2. Die-cut border from white cardstock; ink bottom edges brown and adhere to card front as shown. Doodle along top of border using fine-tip pen.

3. Using brown ink, stamp bird onto card front as shown. Using black ink, stamp sentiment. Attach pearls between words.

4. Wrap ribbon around card front as shown, tying a knot and trimming ribbon ends at an angle; ink ribbon ends brown. ●

Materials

DiscountCardstock.com cardstock: straw, brilliant white
Impression Obsession stamps: Bird Silhouette Flourish, Express Yourself clear set
Clearsnap ink pads: chalk (chestnut roan), dye (licorice)
Sakura black fine-tip pen
Zva Creative white self-adhesive pearls
May Arts ¾-inch-wide blue/white twill stripes ribbon
Impression Obsession Border Duo 2 die set (#DIE018-V)
Sizzix Big Shot die-cutting machine
McGill corner rounder punch
Sponge
SCRAPBOOK ADHESIVES BY 3L™ permanent adhesive strips

tip

Add a vintage feel by sponging the edges of the card with brown ink.

Thoughts of You

Design by Tami Mayberry

tip

Add texture with elements cut from fabrics.

Materials

Core'dinations cardstock: French roast, cream n sugar
Want2Scrap 7 x 7 fabric sheets: canvas, denim
Pebbles Inc. Thinking of You rub-on sentiment
Gina K. Designs tan button
My Favorite Things fine hemp cord
Sizzix Tattered Florals dies (#656640)
Die-cutting machine
SCRAPBOOK ADHESIVES BY 3L™ adhesive runner
Beacon glue

1. Form a 4 x 9-inch card from brown cardstock.

2. Cut a 3¾ x 8¾-inch piece from tan cardstock; center and adhere to card front.

3. Die-cut a 1-inch Tattered Florals flower from denim and a 3-inch flower from canvas. Layer flowers and adhere to card front as shown.

4. Thread button onto cord; tie ends into a bow. Using glue, attach button to flower center.

5. Add rub-on sentiment to card front. ●

Birthday Balloons

Design by Debby Hughes

Materials
Cardstock: Papertrey Ink (soft
  stone); Neenah (solar white)
Teresa Collins Designs Tell Your
  Story 6 x 6 paper pad
Lil' Inker Designs Flags & Tags
  Dies and Stamp set
Imagine Crafts/Tsukineko VersaFine
  smokey gray ink pad
White self-adhesive pearls
The Twinery cantaloupe baker's twine
Dies: Lil' Inker Designs (Balloon Dies);
  Papertrey Ink (Double-Ended
  Banners Die, #PTD-0066)
Lifestyle Crafts Dainty embossing
  folder set (#EF0004)
Die-cutting and embossing machine
Ranger Glossy Accents adhesive
Stampin' Up! adhesive foam squares

1. Form a 4⅛ x 5½-inch card from white cardstock.

2. Cut a 3⅝ x 5-inch piece from light gray cardstock. Emboss using Dainty embossing folder; center and attach to card front using foam squares.

3. Stamp sentiment onto white cardstock. Die-cut a 4¾ x ½-inch Double-Ended Banner around sentiment; attach banner to card front as shown using foam squares and allowing ends of banner to extend past card edges.

4. Die-cut two Balloons from patterned papers. Attach baker's twine for balloon strings using glue. Attach balloons to card front as shown using foam squares; secure balloon strings with glue.

5. Embellish card front with pearls. ●

If your patterned paper is a little on the thin side, back the paper with a piece of cardstock before die-cutting to give the die cut strength and stability.

Fill white space with embossing and a subtle change of color.

Most Likely to Succeed

Design by Laura Williams

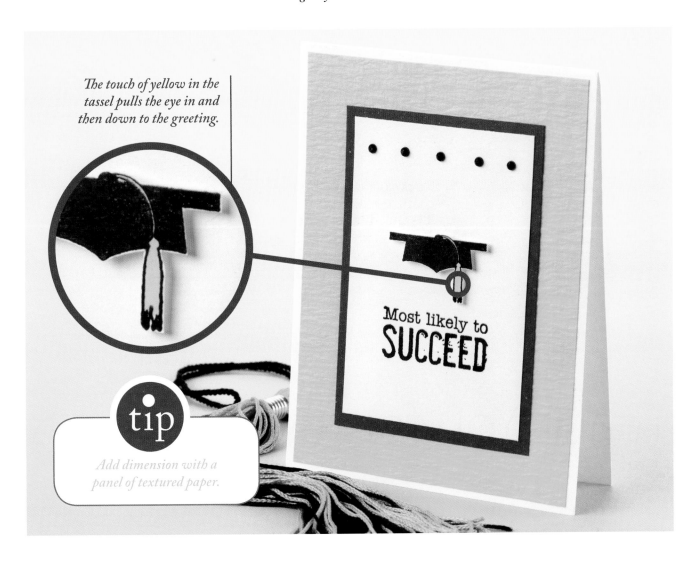

The touch of yellow in the tassel pulls the eye in and then down to the greeting.

tip

Add dimension with a panel of textured paper.

Most likely to
SUCCEED

Materials

DiscountCardstock.com cardstock: brilliant white, posh yellow crepe, posh café satin sparkle
Unity Stamp Co. stamp sets: A to Z Coordinates, Smarty Pants
Clearsnap Mix'd Media Inx black pigment ink pad
Clearsnap Top Boss black embossing powder
ShinHan Art Touch Twin marker: Y35
Want2Scrap black self-adhesive gems
Embossing heat tool
EK Success adhesive foam squares
Close To My Heart glue pen

1. Form a 4¼ x 5½-inch card from white cardstock.

2. Cut a 4 x 5¼-inch piece from yellow cardstock; center and adhere to card front.

3. Cut a 3½ x 4¾-inch piece from white cardstock. Stamp sentiment onto cardstock as shown; sprinkle embossing powder over words and heat-emboss. Attach rhinestones across top of cardstock panel as shown.

4. Stamp mortarboard onto white cardstock; heat-emboss in the same manner as before. Color tassel with yellow marker. Cut out mortarboard and attach to cardstock panel as shown using foam squares.

5. Adhere panel to dark brown sparkle cardstock; trim, leaving a small border. Center and adhere to card front as shown. ●

Cupcake Celebration

Design by Tami Mayberry

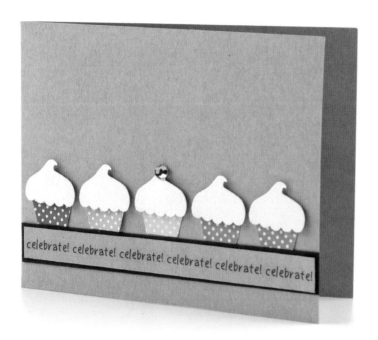

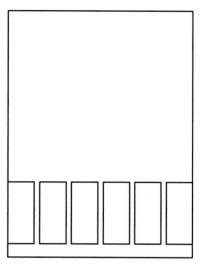

Inspired by card on page 24

Sources: *Cardstock from Gina K. Designs and Core'dinations; Soup Staples II patterned papers from Jillibean Soup; cupcake punch from Fiskars; border sticker from SRM Stickers; rhinestone from Want2Scrap; adhesive foam squares from SCRAPBOOK ADHESIVES BY 3L™.*

Thank You for Your Kindness

Design by Tami Mayberry

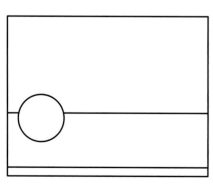

Inspired by card on page 10

Sources: *Cardstock from Gina K. Designs and Core'dinations; stamps and button from Gina K. Designs; ink pad from Clearsnap Inc.; rhinestones from Bo-Bunny Press.*

Celebrate

Design by Tami Mayberry

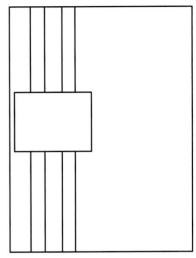

Inspired by card on page 13

Sources: *Cardstock and embellishment from Core'dinations; Soup Staples II patterned paper from Jillibean Soup; ribbon from May Arts Ribbon.*

With Heartfelt Thanks

Design by Tami Mayberry

Inspired by card on page 29

Sources: *Cardstock from Core'dinations; Circles (#657551), Scallop Circles (#657552) and Mini Hearts (#657212) dies from Sizzix; Simple Hearts stamp set from Gina K. Designs; ink pad from Clearsnap Inc.; rhinestones from Want2Scrap; adhesive foam squares from SCRAPBOOK ADHESIVES BY 3L™.*

A Warm Hello

Design by Tami Mayberry

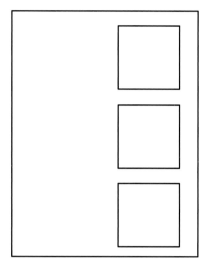

Inspired by card on page 36

Sources: *Cardstock from Core'dinations; patterned paper from Echo Park Paper Co.; Simple Snowflake stamp set from Gina K. Designs; ink pad from Clearsnap Inc.; rhinestones from Want2Scrap; adhesive foam squares from SCRAPBOOK ADHESIVES BY 3L™.*

Happy Harvest

Design by Tami Mayberry

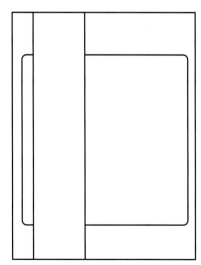

Inspired by card on page 35

Sources: *Cardstock from Core'dinations; patterned paper and sticker from Echo Park Paper Co.; rhinestones from Want2Scrap; ribbon from May Arts Ribbon; corner rounder punch from Fiskars; adhesive foam squares from SCRAPBOOK ADHESIVES BY 3L™.*

Bride to Be

Design by Tami Mayberry

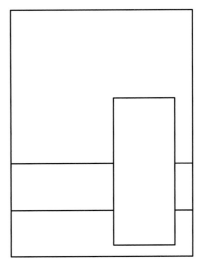

Inspired by card on page 50

Sources: *Cardstock and glitter cardstock from Core'dinations; border sticker from SRM Stickers; dress sticker from Momenta; ribbon from May Arts Ribbon.*

Bright & Happy Day

Design by Tami Mayberry

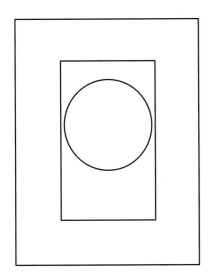

Inspired by card on page 45

Sources: *Cardstock from Core'dinations; Soup Staples II patterned papers from Jillibean Soup; Lighthearted Wishes stamp set from Gina K. Designs; ink pad from Clearsnap Inc.; rhinestone strip from Want2Scrap; corner rounder punch from Fiskars; adhesive foam squares from SCRAPBOOK ADHESIVES BY 3L™.*

Buyer's Guide

3M
(800) 328-6276
www.scotchbrand.com

American Crafts
(801) 226-0747
www.americancrafts.com

A Muse Studio
www.amusestudio.com

Bazzill Basics Paper Inc.
(800) 560-1610
www.bazzillbasics.com

Beacon Adhesives Inc.
(914) 699-3405
www.beaconcreates.com

Bo-Bunny Press
(801) 771-4010
www.bobunny.com

Clear and Simple Stamps
www.clearandsimplestamps.com

Clearsnap Inc.
(800) 448-4862
www.clearsnap.com

Close To My Heart
www.closetomyheart.com

Copic®/Imagination International Inc.
(541) 684-0013
www.copicmarker.com

Core'dinations
www.coredinations.com

Craftwork Cards
www.craftworkcards.co.uk

Creative Memories
www.creativememories.com

Darcie's LLC
(800) 945-3980
www.darciesllc.com

DiscountCardstock.com
(801) 876-0327
www.discountcardstock.com

Echo Park Paper Co.
(800) 701-1115
www.echoparkpaper.com

EK Success
www.eksuccessbrands.com

Fiskars
(866) 348-5661
www2.fiskars.com

Flower Soft® Inc.
(877) 989-0205
www.flower-soft.com

Gina K. Designs
(608) 838-3258
www.ginakdesigns.com

Hero Arts
(800) 822-HERO (822-4376)
www.heroarts.com

Imagine Crafts/Tsukineko
(425) 883-7733
www.imaginecrafts.com

Impression Obsession Inc.
(877) 259-0905
www.iostamps.com

Jillibean Soup
(888) 212-1177
www.jillibean-soup.com

JustRite Papercraft Inc.
(866) 405-6414
www.justritestampers.com

Kaisercraft
(888) 684-7147
www.kaisercraft.com.au

Lawn Fawn
www.lawnfawn.com

Lifestyle Crafts
(866) 212-3214
http://lifestylecrafts.com

Lil' Inker Designs
www.lilinkerdesigns.com

Martha Stewart Crafts
www.eksuccessbrands.com/marthastewartcrafts

May Arts Ribbon
(203) 637-8366
www.mayarts.com

McGill Inc.
(800) 982-9884
www.mcgillinc.com

Memory Box
www.memoryboxco.com

Momenta
(800) 448-6656
http://momenta.com

My Favorite Things
www.mftstamps.com

My Mind's Eye
(800) 665-5116
www.mymindseye.com

Neenah Paper Inc.
(800) 994-5993
www.neenahpaper.com

October Afternoon
(866) 513-5553
www.octoberafternoon.com

Offray
(800) 237-9425
www.offray.com

The Paper Loft
(801) 254-1961
www.paperloft.com

Paper Smooches
(623) 533-3776
www.papersmoochesstamps.com

Papertrey Ink
www.papertreyink.com

Pebbles Inc.
(801) 226-0747
www.pebblesinc.com

Pizzazz Aplenty
(765) 883-5279
www.pizzazzaplenty.blogspot.com

Prima Marketing Inc.
(909) 627-5532
www.primamarketinginc.com

Ranger Industries Inc.
(732) 389-3535
www.rangerink.com

Sakura of America
www.sakuraofamerica.com

Scor-Pal Products
(877) 629-9908
www.scor-pal.com

SCRAPBOOK ADHESIVES BY 3L™
www.scrapbook-adhesives.com

ShinHan USA Inc.
www.shinhanart.com

Simple Stories
www.simplestories.com

Sizzix
(877) 355-4766
www.sizzix.com

Spellbinders™ Paper Arts
(888) 547-0400
www.spellbinderspaperarts.com

SRM Stickers
(800) 323-9589
www.srmpress.com

Stampin' Up!
(800) STAMP UP (782-6787)
www.stampinup.com

The Stamps of Life
www.stephaniebarnardstamps.com

Teresa Collins Designs
(877) 417-3195
www.teresacollinsdesigns.com

Tombow USA
www.tombowusa.com

The Twinery
http://thetwinery.com

Uchida of America Corp.
(800) 541-5877
www.uchida.com

Unity Stamp Co.
(877) 862-2329
www.unitystampco.com

Waltzingmouse Stamps
www.waltzingmousestamps.com

Want2Scrap
(260) 740-2976
www.Want2Scrap.com

We R Memory Keepers
(877) PICKWER (742-5937)
www.weronthenet.com

Zva Creative
(801) 243-9281
www.zvacreative.com

The Buyer's Guide listings are provided as a service to our readers and should not be considered an endorsement from this publication.

Annie's®

Clean & Simple Cards is published by Annie's, 306 East Parr Road, Berne, IN 46711. Printed in USA. Copyright © 2013 Annie's. All rights reserved. This publication may not be reproduced in part or in whole without written permission from the publisher.

RETAIL STORES: If you would like to carry this pattern book or any other Annie's publication, visit AnniesWSL.com.

Every effort has been made to ensure that the instructions in this pattern book are complete and accurate. We cannot, however, take responsibility for human error, typographical mistakes or variations in individual work. Please visit AnniesCustomerCare.com to check for pattern updates.

ISBN: 978-1-59635-587-3

1 2 3 4 5 6 7 8 9